THE
Archive Photographs
SERIES

PUBS OF THE OLD STROUD BREWERY

Phoenix Inn, Thrupp. This inn, probably contemporary with the adjacent Phoenix Iron Works, is seen undergoing refurbishment *c.* 1910. The plain brick building tenanted by George Cullimore (see page 36) has been rendered and now sports an attractive oriel window and elaborate signboard (note similarities with the Post Office Inn). This cleverly posed photograph shows foreman, tradesmen and the heavy wooden scaffolding and ladders typical of the period. For some years after the First World War the licensee was Wilf Budding, a distant relative of Edwin Budding, the inventor of the lawn mower. Since its closure the premises have been used for retail purposes. (Photograph by Lockyer)

THE
Archive Photographs
SERIES

PUBS OF THE OLD STROUD BREWERY

Compiled by
Wilfred Merrett

First published 1996

The Chalford Publishing Company
St Mary's Mill, Chalford,
Stroud, Gloucestershire, GL6 8NX

ISBN 0 7524 0673 6

Typesetting and origination by
The Chalford Publishing Company
Printed in Great Britain by
Redwood Books, Trowbridge

Worth Stopping For. In this rare advertisement card the cyclists appear to have strayed far from the Cotswolds, judging by the architecture.

Contents

Acknowledgements

I am most grateful to all of the following who have made this book possible by contributing material, information and advice:

Keith Apperley, Howard Beard, Doreen Burr, Mrs Close, Mary Cowley, John Dennis, William Didcot, Tim Edgell, Keith Fyleman (Peckham of Stroud Ltd), Brian Frith, Ken Grey, Eunice Guy, Eileen Halliday, Elizabeth Harvey, Mike Hawkes, Olive Hughes, Mrs Jordan, Vera Kilmister, Anne Makemson, Lily Mason, Steve Mills, Mick Minett, Clive Olpin, Nigel Paterson, Oliver Pike, Ted Prince, Nick Redman (Whitbread Archivist), Beryl Ridley, David Russell, Allan Smith, Ivan Smith, Marion Tuck, Philip Walmsley and the Stroud Local History Society, Staff at Cheltenham, Gloucester and Stroud Reference Libraries.

Most of all I am indebted to my wife and daughter for practical help, patience and constant encouragement.

Bibliography

P.H. Fisher: *Notes and Recollections of Stroud*, J. Elliott, 1871.
S. Gardiner, L. Padin: *Stroud and the Five Valleys*, Alan Sutton Publishing Ltd, 1984.
A.E. Keys: *A History of Eastington*, Stroud News & Journal Ltd, 1964.
J. Libby: *Twenty Years History of Stroud 1870-1890.*
B. Mills: *Portrait of Nailsworth*, B.A. Hathaway 1985.
M. Rudd: *Historical Records of Bisley with Lypiatt*, 1937.
J. Shipman: *Bisley A Cotswold Village Remembered 1860-1945*, Chantry Press 1991.
Victoria County History, *The History of the County of Gloucester*, Volume Xl 1976.

Introduction

Following the acquisition of a number of smaller breweries during the early years of this century the Directors of The Stroud Brewery decided that there should be a photographic record of all their public houses. This commission was accepted by Henry Lockyer, a local photographer, who operated from his private house at The Knoll, Leonard Stanley.

Lockyer is recalled by the older generation as a pipe smoker, usually attired in plus fours, and despite lameness attributable to a gunshot wound, he rode long distances on his Pedersen bicycle. He probably adopted this mode of transport to carry his photographic paraphernalia when in 1910, or thereabouts, he set off to record not only the local pubs but inns as far afield as Minety in Wiltshire and Blakeney in The Forest of Dean. In total he photographed over a hundred pubs, most of which are reproduced in this book. It is not clear just what use was made of these photographs but subsequently they were filed away in a drawer and virtually forgotten for some fifty years. Following the Whitbread takeover, brewing ceased in 1957, staff cleared their desks and much paperwork was destroyed, but fortunately these photographs survived and eventually came into my possession.

It is apparent from Lockyer's work that he was an extremely competent photographer. He clearly enjoyed portraying not only the brewery properties but also the people concerned with them. In other words he liked his photographs to be 'animated' by the presence of the landlord, his family, his customers and often his animals. If workmen were present they were included along with the tools of their trade, carefully posed to make allowance for the slower exposure times then required. In some cases where inns were being refurbished 'before and after' photographs were taken, but in general the premises were recorded just as Lockyer found them with little preparation or tidying up.

As suggested by the photographs, the public houses of the Edwardian period were far removed from the spruce sanitised establishments of today, nevertheless the country inns in particular had a simple charm as yet unspoiled by the arrival of the motor car. The sterile car parks surrounding modern pubs often occupy land that would have been cultivated by the landlord to supplement his relatively meagre income. Virtually all male preserves, these were the taverns frequented by Cecil Sharp in his quest for old English folk songs, and George Borrow and even Dr Johnson might have felt at home in some of them. Patrons of what were often beer, or possibly cider houses, would find little in the way of food other than a sandwich or a pickled egg, although the larger inns might have offered cooked meals and accommodation for visitors to the increasingly popular Cotswolds. The town pubs varied from the basic 'spit and sawdust' to the custom built inns complete with elaborate tiled facades and decorative frosted glass so beloved by the Victorians. Urban landlords had less need to seek part time jobs and in the photographs they tend to present a smarter appearance than their rural counterparts.

During the 1930s and early 1950s further photographs were taken by Edwin Peckham and William Adams for Stroud Brewery publications and some of these have been included, together with a number of old postcard views featuring pubs. The reproduced inn signs are the work of Mike Hawkes, former Stroud Brewery sign writer and the letterheads and printed ephemera derive from material donated to The Stroud Local History Society.

Obviously the short captions in this book cannot do justice to the history surrounding many of the inns featured and as my collection represents less than fifty percent of The Stroud Brewery properties there are many omissions. In some cases information has been sparse, but landlords, regulars, ex brewery employees and local historians have always been willing to help. A pinch of salt has proved necessary in some instances and I have reluctantly omitted certain references to Queen Elizabeth I, Oliver Cromwell and Judge Jeffreys, who allegedly patronised some of the older establishments! The research has involved many miles of relatively abstemious pub crawling and meetings with numerous interesting and knowledgeable people, none more so than the 92 year old gentleman in Gloucester whose father manufactured and supplied clay pipes to the local hostelries for a few pence a gross !

Wilf Merrett
July 1996

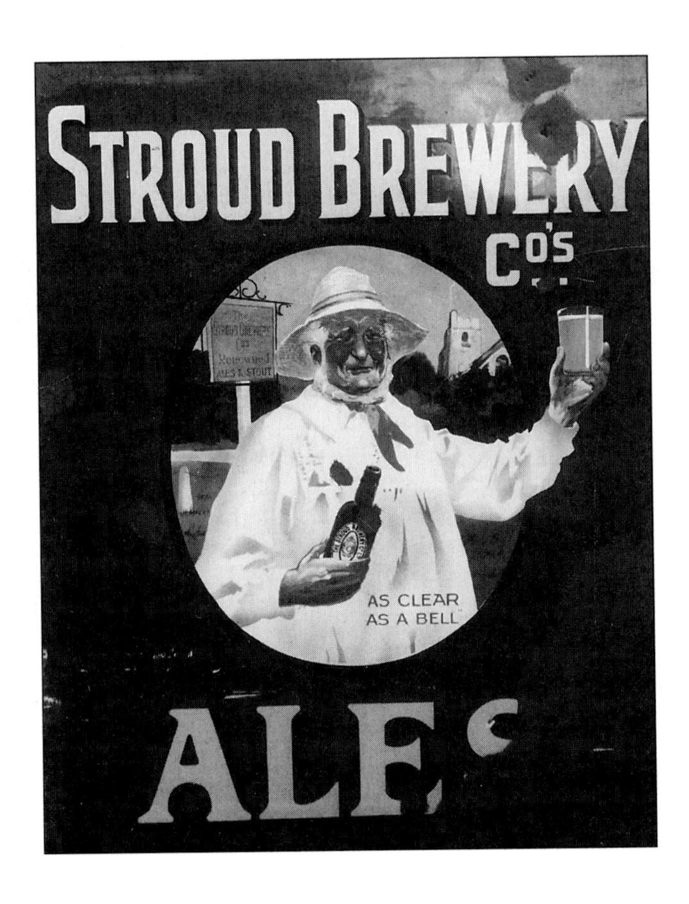

One

Stroud Brewery Co. Ltd

From small beginnings in the eighteenth century the Stroud Brewery grew into a successful business and became a limited company in 1888 when extensive premises were erected at Merrywalks and Rowcroft. During the next half century many smaller breweries at Tetbury, Minchinhampton, Malmesbury and Marlborough were absorbed, but the major coup was undoubtedly in 1928 when Godsell's Salmon Springs Brewery, the chief competitor, was acquired together with its valuable Callowell water supply. Thus in 1928 Stroud Brewery owned no less than 460 inns, hotels and off licences.

In 1959 the Stroud Brewery merged with the Cheltenham and Hereford Breweries to become West Country Brewery Holdings, and in 1967 following the new company's acquisition by Whitbread, brewing in Stroud came to an end. The Rowcroft premises including the fine Cotswold stone office block erected by W.F. Drew of Chalford, and the dominant 1901 chimney stack, were demolished, and the site is now largely occupied by the Stroud and Swindon Building Society.

Early Brewery advertising card. This postcard produced early this century advertises beer costing less than one new penny a pint.

Stroud Brewery. A general view of the Stroud Brewery as seen from Cainscross Road. Note the narrowness of Merrywalks and the open stream. (Photograph by Peckham).

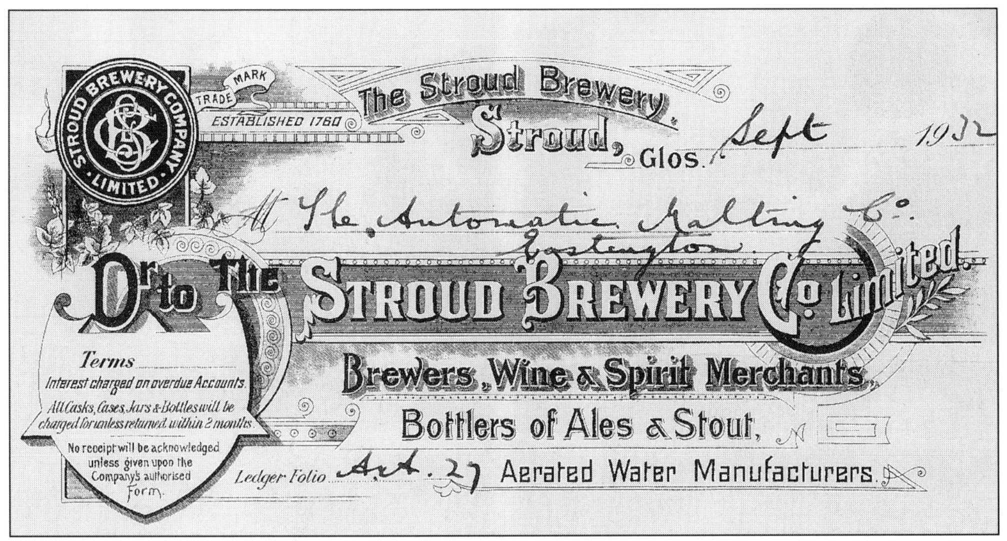

Stroud Brewery letterhead. This elaborate letterhead was used by the Brewery for at least thirty years.

CHEAPER ALE.

The Stroud Brewery Co., Ltd.,

will supply a

SPECIAL ALE

for the

HAYMAKING and HARVEST SEASONS, 1931,

known as **"H.A."** at the following prices—

	£	s.	d.
Pin	0	7	6
Firkin	0	15	0
Kilderkin	1	10	0
Barrel	3	0	0
Hogshead	4	10	0

Less usual discount for cash 1 month.

Prompt Delivery.

THE BREWERY, STROUD.

'Phone No. 463 (2 lines).

Cheaper Ale.

Delivering in Gloucester. The original Stroud Brewery motor lorry is shown delivering beer to the Black Dog Inn, Gloucester in the early 1920s.

New Acquisition. This fine Thornycroft lorry is posed for its pre-delivery photograph in the works yard at Basingstoke in 1930. The Stroud Brewery lorries with their polished aluminium bonnets, lavish chrome and bright primary colours made an impressive sight when lined up outside the Rowcroft premises.

Two

Stroud

Stroud may have possessed as many as fifty inns and messuages (off licenses) at the turn of the century, and, in 1928 the Stroud Brewery alone owned thirty such premises in the town.

Twenty four of these establishments are shown in the following photographs, which unfortunately do not include some of the lesser known pubs such as The Hope Inn, The Half Moon or the long forgotten Star in Tower Hill (Parliament Street). Of these no less than ten stood within a stone's throw of the Cross, including The Corn Exchange, Kings Head, Crown, Bedford Arms, Duke of York, Lamb, Swan, Golden Fleece, Orange Tree and Half Moon. A few years earlier this list would have included The Corn Hall Hotel in the Shambles, and The Rising Sun, The New George and The Wellington Arms, all in Nelson Street.

Few of these inns remain today, and the survivors offer a much higher standard of service and hygiene, but so often at the expense of their character and individuality.

Imperial Hotel. The architect of this impressive building was Benjamin Bucknall, better known as the designer of Woodchester Park Mansion. Prior to 1900 the premises were extended and stables erected opposite the street entrance creating 'one of the most comfortable and well conducted hotels in the West of England', according to Libby. The Stroud Brewery purchased the premises from Regina Court Ltd for £25,000 in 1949, and the following year the Queen, then Princess Elizabeth, met civic leaders in the hotel lounge during a fleeting visit to the town. (Photo by W.D. Moss)

The Greyhound Inn. This inn, prominently situated at the top of Gloucester Street, dates from the eighteenth century, but was completely rebuilt by Godsells in 1903, and their malt shovel motif can be seen above the greyhound. Note that the postcard refers to the 'new corner'. Some readers may recall Big Tom Bacon, the Welsh landlord and his pretty daughter, Myra. A subsequent licensee is reputed to have employed seven Irish barmaids! During 1948 one regular, Jimmy Sands, reached the semi finals of the *News of the World* darts championship. (Hartmann postcard)

Ye Olde Painswick Inn. This handsome hostelry does not appear to be particularly 'olde'; in fact the present building was created in 1896. It is now being adapted as residential accommodation for young people.

The Green Dragon. During Victorian times, four public houses were sited in King Street, namely The Royal George, The Chequers, The Golden Heart and The Green Dragon. The Golden Heart was a prosperous concern where Mr Bluett, the Inland Revenue Officer had his premises. This gentleman also acted as a parcels agent for the Midland Railway. The adjoining and dilapidated Green Dragon whose first recorded licensee in 1820 was William Merrett, had a rapid succession of landlords. Completely rebuilt by Godsells early this century, the upper part of the once elegant façade can still be seen above Halford's shop premises.

The Post Office Inn. The name of this inn derives from the fact that the building housed Stroud's first Post Office from 1857 to 1886. Accessible from both George Street and Russell Street it was, according to the *Gloucestershire Guide* of 1928 'a popular calling house which caters for customers in an admirable manner'. Following its closure some years ago it has been used as offices by The Britannic Assurance Co. (Photograph by Lockyer).

Arnold Perrett & Co Ltd, Wickwar. This company was actually acquired by The Cheltenham Brewery in 1924, but later became part of West Country Holdings. The retail wine and spirits shop shown at the bottom of the High Street in 1969 is now a part of Andrews Estate Agents.

Swan Inn. The original Swan Inn stood in the High Street, opposite the Shambles, and, following its closure, the present Swan Inn was erected in Union Street in 1822. Its most noted feature is the gallows sign, which spans the street, one of the few remaining. The Inland Revenue Office occupied by the Collector, William Rayner, was based at the Swan Inn in 1859. It is noteworthy that similar congenial surroundings were afforded to his predecessor, Mr Bluett, at The Golden Heart. The Swan has benefited from recent pedestrianisation, and tables and chairs are placed outside the inn for customers on sunny days. (Photograph by Lockyer).

The original Bedford Arms had been founded as The Marlborough Head on the north side of the High Street in 1776. Situated just about where the Trustee Savings Bank now stands, it projected some nine feet into the street. In the 1830s the inn was renamed The Bedford Arms in honour of Lord John Russell's father, the Duke of Bedford, and following its closure in 1854 the sign was adopted by another public house at the corner of High Street and Church street. The photograph was taken between 1907 and 1914 when Charles Hall was the landlord. More recently Mr Cyril (Cocker) Wilson was licensee for many years prior to its closure some thirty odd years ago. (Photograph by Lockyer).

This amusing poster was a familiar sight on local advertisement hoarding in prewar days

The Corn Exchange Hotel. Following the demolition of a malt house in 1815, a handsome block of stone property was erected on the north side of the High Street where the electrical goods shop of Lewis and Co now stands. These premises incorporated a large public room which was converted into a Corn Exchange in 1861; this name was also given to a new public house sited in Exchange Buildings, which may have replaced the former White Hart. The last licensee, Reg Boobyer, left in 1959 before the site was redeveloped. The inn and the adjoining shop were sold by The Stroud Brewery for £4,000. (Photograph by Lockyer).

Horse and Groom, The Leazes. With at least five pubs in close proximity it is hardly surprising that only one, The Horse and Groom, survives. At one time the haunt of local card sharpers and allegedly 'open all hours', the premises and surroundings have been much improved in recent years, including the incorporation of the adjoining brewmaster's cottage into the main building. 'Frank', a former regular with vocal ambitions, was inclined to inflict outbursts of Italian opera on unsuspecting customers. (Photograph by Lockyer).

The New Inn, Lower Street. The name of the landlord is not decipherable in this photograph, but may be Arthur Seabourne who was there in 1907. A predecessor, Thomas Hallewell, performed the rather incompatible activities of paperhanger and beer retailer. For many years the inn was the headquarters of the Stroud Angling Club, a former landlord, Charles Peyton was Vice President. E.J. May was the last licensee before the pub became a private residence. (Photograph by Lockyer).

The Spread Eagle. Like most properties on the north side of Bisley Old Road, The Spread Eagle was removed for road widening in the 1960s. Rupert Clift was the landlord for many years, and trade was particularly good during the last war when the American GIs, stationed at Lypiatt Park and the old workhouse, often drank the pub dry. A small adjacent shop had a variety of uses, from faggots and peas in the 1920s, to shoe repairs and later radio and electrical repairs carried out by a gentleman called Tommy Tipple. (Photograph by W.F. Lee).

Sundial Inn. Probably built soon after the creation of the new London Road in 1814 this inn closed many years ago, but happily the sundial still remains. The object in the top right hand corner is an inn sign not a satellite dish!

Bisley House Inn. In 1856 Middle Street possessed two beer retailers, one wine and spirit retailer and an inn known as The Sydney Arms. There is no apparent record of Ye Olde Bisley House, although this establishment is referred to in the Brewery's *Gloucestershire Guide* of 1928 as one of the oldest licensed houses in the town. It is understood that the present Bisley House Inn dating from c. 1899 was built to replace an earlier inn which still stands as an adjacent private house. This inn may also have been known as Ye Olde Bisley House, having changed its name from The Sydney Arms.

Butchers Arms, Stroud. This inn in Acre Street (less than one hundred yards from its namesake in Parliament Street) is now a private residence. William Watts, licensee for many years prior to 1907, was succeeded by his widow, Henrietta. Ten years later the property was valued at £695. Probably the best known licensee in recent years was Victor Bingle. (Photograph by Lockyer).

The Fountain Inn. Following the closure of The Prince of Wales, the Fountain is the only inn serving the Slad Road and Uplands Area. The building appears to be of late Victorian vintage, and the first recorded landlord was Issac Englishman in 1896. The square entrance porch standing between the two bay windows was removed many years ago. The photograph suggests that the pub may have been a mecca for the local cycling fraternity. (Photograph by Lockyer).

The Orange Tree Inn. Bill Bartlett, seen in this photograph, was a well known and popular landlord of this typical Top of the Town pub for well over thirty years drawing his customers from far and wide. The Orange Tree was demolished following its closure in 1958 for road and car park improvements. Its 'Tower Hill' neighbour The Half Moon survives as a private house.

The Target Inn, Stroud. This inn takes its name from the shooting range in the Horns Valley used by the Stroud Volunteers during the last century. It was exceedingly popular with the GIs billeted in the old Stroud workhouse during the war, but parking problems probably contributed to its decline in recent years. It is now purely residential.

The Leopard Inn. Nothing now remains of The Leopard Inn which stood just above the Cotswold Playhouse in Parliament Street. The inn featured prominently in darts and cribbage competitions, and the landlord, Percy Cowley, was singles winner in the Stroud and District Cribbage League. Customers of this beer house were drawn mainly from the immediate neighbourhood. Several took part in the first Stroud International Brick Throwing Contest which took place in the adjacent recreation field. (Photograph by Lockyer).

The Bell Inn, Stroud. This unusually shaped building was conveniently sited to provide refreshment for travellers using the Great Western and Midland Railway stations. The Stroud Brewery acquired The Bell in 1889, hardly surprising as it was just across the road. In recent years the premises, now a hotel, have been much improved and extended by Luciano Magalotti who also owns The Clothiers Arms.

Percy Cowley. The landlord as depicted by the gifted local cartoonist 'Echo' Organ. Mr Cowley was at the Leopard from 1944 until its closure in 1968.

Chapel Street Off Licence. William Barnes stands outside his off-licence in this ninety year old photograph. Customers collected their beer in a variety of containers. The writer experienced his first taste when a young Chapel Street friend was sent to replenish his father's jug and we both sampled the contents. The word 'Entire' shown on the sign board refers to a mixture of ale and porter popular at the time. (Photograph by Lockyer).

The Kings Arms Inn. This ancient Wallbridge pub was demolished some years ago to make way for the extension to T. Butt and Sons premises. Together with the nearby Ship and Anchor Inns, The Kings Arms would have been popular with nineteenth-century canal workers. Albert Smith, the licensee in 1907, also ran the nearby refreshment rooms, and Mark Merrett, an ancestor of the writer was in business as an umbrella maker in the next cottage. A well-known landlord, Harry Minett, managed the pub in postwar years before moving to The Rose at Paganhill.

Middle Street Off Licence. This off-licence was one of two situated in Middle Street Uplands. During the 1930s it was managed by Mr and Mrs Townsend, the former resembling King George V with his Van Dyke beard. After the war the premises were extended to create a mini market but this has since closed and the property is now residential. (Photograph by Lockyer).

Clothiers Arms, Bath Road. The inn is believed to have been converted from a small cottage in the late nineteenth century. The architect was P.R. Morley Horder who was also responsible for the renovation of The Prince Albert. The present car park and beer garden are built on the site of Mowmead House which was separated from the inn by Monkey Lane. Behind Mowmead House was a workshop where tents were manufactured, particularly during the First World War. The Bennett family were licensees for three generations, over sixty years, during which time further improvements were carried out. More recently the present owner, Luciano Magalotti, has extended the premises to include a spacious and popular restaurant. This photograph shows a rear view of the premises, probably commissioned by the Brewery, prior to carrying out alterations. (Photograph by Lockyer).

Oddfellows Arms, Summer Street. This unusual pub with its crenellated bays closed for some thirty years ago and is now hardly recognisable. Before the last war the tenant was a Mr Skinner, who, despite only having one arm was a part time farmer as well as a publican. For many years the Oddfellows was the headquarters of the Stroud Pigeon Fanciers Club. The birds were transported hundreds of miles by lorry from this central point. Part of the premises was used as a shop and I well remember buying sweets and fizzy drinks there in the 1930s.

The Fleece Inn, Lightpill. Competition must have been rife between The Fleece and the adjacent Cyprus which sold Cheltenham ales. Both inns probably relied on workers from nearby factories for much of their trade. This scene is enlivened by the smocked landlord feeding the chickens watched by his dog and cat. (Photograph by Lockyer).

The Golden Cross Inn. This old hostelry gave its name to the notorious crossroads a mile out of town towards Nailsworth. The inn which originally had a beer licence remained in the same family for many years. Mr and Mrs Taylor were licensees from 1911 to 1933 followed by their daughter Mrs Bateman who remained there until 1956. There were then rapid changes of tenancy until the premises were acquired by the County Council for road improvements. This photograph shows the single storey extension and the adjoining cottages which included a small grocery shop run by Mr and Mrs Price. During the last war the Stroud section of the Stroud Brewery sign was removed for security reasons.

The Rose Inn, Paganhill. This photograph was taken in the 1950s when the premises were modernised and extended to include the adjoining cottages. Despite its appearance this inn was recorded as early as 1822 and during the renovations a tricorn hat was discovered. After leaving The Kings Arms in 1952 Harry Minett became licensee of The Rose and it remained in the family for many years. Further internal alterations have been made but the popular skittle alley still remains. (Photograph by Peckham).

The White Horse Inn, Cainscross. The licensee of The White Horse in 1954 was Richard Darke who combined the activities of landlord and butcher. The *Stroud Press* of 30 June 1854 carried this advertisement: 'WHITE HORSE COMMERCIAL INN, CAINSCROSS BY R. DARKE. NEAT FLY, PHAETON AND SADDLE HORSES FOR HIRE. CHOICEST WINES AND SPIRITS. THE HOUSE WARMING DINNER ON MONDAY JULY 3rd AT 4 O'CLOCK. TICKETS 2/6 EACH. R.D. CONTINUES TO CARRY ON THE TRADE OF BUTCHER.' Rumour has it that the building is haunted following a suicide in Darke's butchers shop. Rose Chandler shown as licensee in the photograph remained at the White Horse for many years after the death of her husband in about 1910. (Photograph by Peckham).

The Spring Inn, Cainscross. This postcard, published by W.G. Andrews, probably dates from around 1920 when the inn was valued at £600. The building remains but the road has been extensively altered.

Bridge Inn, Dudbridge. This old inn with its unusual windows was popular with the local factory and canal workers. It is recalled that a former licensee, Joe Symonds, was determined to keep an orderly house. He would not tolerate swearing or bad behaviour and kept a shotgun inside the case of a grandfather clock to emphasise his authority. Joe, who sported a distinctive beard and moustache, also kept cattle in the adjoining field.. The inn was subject to flooding and on occasion the regulars kept dry by standing on boxes. Henry Gay, featured in the photograph, was licensee during 1907/1908. (Photograph by Lockyer).

Bridge Inn Summer Outing 1928. Joe Symonds, the landlord, poses proudly with his customers before embarking on a charabanc outing. For Gilbert Haliday, third from the left, it was a trip not to be repeated; 'we seemed to stop at every pub!' The 'men only' group also includes Joe Bullock the canal supervisor and Freddy Bassett who was in charge of Dudbridge Lock. The driver was Jimmy Cant.

The Gardeners Rest. This impressive modern building with its green pantiled roof was erected by Stroud Brewery in 1956 to serve the needs of the growing Cashes Green estates. Apart from the Robinswood Inn at Matson this was the only new public house commissioned by the Stroud Brewery since the last war. The architect was H.R. Robinson and the first landlord was Eric Tuckwell who opened the doors to the public on Wednesday 15 August 1956. (Photograph by Peckham).

The Railway Inn, Dudbridge. This inn, recently renamed The Junction, formerly derived much of its trade from the railway workers at the nearby Dudbridge station. Now defoliated, refurbished and displaying a symbolic railway signal it is a popular venue for young people with a taste for live pop music. (Photograph by Lockyer).

Prince Albert Inn. this early postcard shows the inn before its enlargement during the early part of this century. The architect responsible was P.R. Morley-Harder who also redesigned the Clothier's Arms. Situated near the popular walking and leisure area of Rodborough Common the 1930 licensee P.G. Poole offered 'teas and light refreshments at short notice'. He also supplemented his income by hiring out his 'high class' Wolseley saloon for weddings, dances etc. The premises are described in the Stroud Brewery's schedule of properties as inn, stables, four cottages and bowling green; the latter still in frequent use.

Inn Sign. This impressive sign was the work of Mike Hawkes.

Kings Head Inn, Kingscourt. Situated in the oldest part of Kingscourt this inn, part of which dates back to the seventeenth century, has been extensively altered internally on the open plan principle. As can be seen from the photograph the area in front of the pub was thoroughly cultivated and Harry Weaving, landlord in the 1930s, sold his garden produce and other foodstuffs to supplement his income. Further up 'The Street' stands the former Boot Inn c. 1703 which was also a bakery and in nearby Bowl Hill the sign of The Nag's Head is still legible on a house now named 'Laburnam'. (Photograph by Lockyer).

KINGSCOURT

Nr. STROUD.

VALUABLE FREEHOLD PROPERTY

DAVIS, CHAMPION & PAYNE

will SELL BY AUCTION at the

"WHITE HORSE INN," CAINSCROSS,

On TUESDAY, NOVEMBER 10th, 1931,

punctually at **6.30 p.m.** in one lot,

The valuable Stone-built and Tiled OFF-LICENSED PREMISES, for many years in the occupation of the late Mr. G. Chapman, and known as

"THE BOOT INN,"

KINGSCOURT, containing: Passage, Living Room with oven grate, Cellar, Pantry, Three Bedrooms, Attic, W.C., Washhouse, and Coal House. Together with

TWO Stone-built and Tiled COTTAGES

adjoining. The first contains: Living Room, Bedroom, Landing Room, Attic and Scullery, and the second contains: Living Room with oven grate, Bedroom and Attic, W.C. for joint use of the two cottages. Let respectively to Messrs. P. Glassonbury and A. Bendall, on monthly tenancies, at rentals amounting to £15 : 10 : 0 per annum Tenants paying rates.

Good Productive Gardens.

Company's Gas. Main Drainage.

NOTE. *The washhouse is for the joint use of all three houses, and Mr. Glassonbury also has the right to draw water from the large rain water tank at the side of "The Boot Inn."*

The Auctioneers would like to draw especial attention to this Sale. The property is situate in a well populated district, and the business is capable of considerable extension.

Vacant Possession of the "BOOT INN" on completion of Purchase

Further particulars may be had of the AUCTIONEERS, 16, Kendrick Street, Stroud; or of

MESSRS. HEELAS & SHEPPARD,
Solicitors, Rowcroft, Stroud.

Walter Collins, Printer, Stroud

Sale details of the Boot Inn.

Three
Chalford Valley

Bowbridge, at the head of the valley, was served by several inns or beer houses. The British Oak completely regenerated by Jenny Bircher is still with us but the Canal Tavern and The New Inn (delicensed in 1892) have long since disappeared.

Following the closure of the Fountain and, more recently, the Forester's Arms and the Malakoff only The Waggon and Horses continues to provide hospitality in Thrupp, whilst Brimscombe relies on The King and Castle, The Kings Arms and The Ship. An ancestor of the writer, John Merrett was for short time landlord of The Nelson, but, having broken his leg whilst endeavouring to eject a drunk decided that inn keeping was not his forte.

Of the former nine pubs in Chalford which would have served the canal or factory workers only the Red Lion remains. Fortunately a number of these old premises have been converted to form desirable homes, often with names that give a clue to their original purpose.

Forester's Arms, Claypits, Thrupp. Situated high above Thrupp, this former beer house is believed to date back to the sixteenth century. In summer months it provided a good excuse for a pleasurable walk from Stroud through the Horn's Valley, but sadly it closed its doors in the 1960s and is now a desirable cottage residence. Mr and Mrs Albert Pearce were popular tenants until 1962, when the licence was transferred to Albert Pimm, a local postman. Charles Peyton the landlord when the photograph was taken c. 1910, may have subsequently moved to the New Inn, Lower Street. (Photograph by Lockyer).

Malakoff Inn, Thrupp. Like its namesake in Ebley, this inn presumably dating from the 1850s, was named after an old Russian fortress captured and destroyed by the allies during the Crimean War. During the tenure of Ken and Mabel Baxter a wooden extension was added at the side of the inn to create a family room, this being known locally as Noah's Ark. The inn closed some years ago and is now privately owned.

Phoenix Inn, Thrupp. It is interesting to compare this photograph of the Phoenix Inn with that of the same building following refurbishment *c.* 1910. The card in the right-hand window advertises Prince cider. (Photograph by Lockyer).

Waggon & Horses, Thrupp. This, the only surviving Thrupp public house, is late Victorian, and in 1935 came to prominence when a skittle alley was installed behind the building which involved the diversion of a footpath. John Cousins, licensee for many years including 1910, when this photograph was taken, was succeeded by Jack Cousins (his son?) who, in addition to running the pub, owned an iron foundry in Brimscombe, and was also a partner in the furniture business of Cousins Matthews. An engineering enthusiast, Jack Cousins bought a Sentinel steam lorry, and, having mastered its complexities, instructed a Stroud Brewery driver when the company acquired a similar vehicle. The inn has recently been refurbished and reopened. (Photograph by Lockyer).

Inn sign by Mile Hawkes.

Victoria Hotel, Brimscombe. The proprietor, H. Eddell, also ran horse buses between Chalford and Stonehouse, and hired out charabancs, waggonettes and wedding carriage. In 1904, when Eddell sent this postcard, beer was supplied by the Brimscombe Brewery. The hotel has been renamed the King and Castle, having previously been known as the Railway, and the Hotel Victoria.

Ship Inn, Brimscombe. This inn was probably opened when the Thames and Severn Canal was built, and until at least 1830 was run by members of the Butler family. Sarah Butler (1755-1831) widow of the first proprietor ran the inn after his death and was a founder of Littleworth and Brimscombe Methodist chapels. In 1891 it was owned by Mrs John Ralph and tied to Stroud Brewery. Neighbouring inns that closed include the Yew Tree, The Nelson and the Red Lion. Fortunately, The Ship is still providing traditional hospitality. (Photograph by Lockyer).

Port Inn, Brimscombe. Like the neighbouring Ship Inn, this pub would have served the workers at Brimscombe Port and the nearby factories. The building is now a private house.

Bell Inn, Chalford. This is probably the inn mentioned as being in Bisley parish in 1781, when Joseph Clissold was the victualler. It gives its name to Bell Lock on the Thames and Severn Canal and like the nearby New Red Lion, would have attracted trade from the bargees and canal workers. This inn possessed a large assembly room which was much used, particularly for Chartist meetings in the 1830s when the cloth industry collapsed. During the 1920s the licensee was George Brown, well known locally for his thriving trade in rabbits which he had shot. The inn previously owned by Cooks New Brewery of Tetbury was acquired by the Stroud Brewery in 1913; it was demolished many years ago. (Photograph by Lockyer).

Company's Arms, Chalford. Previously known as Chalford Place, this ornate building was turned into an inn by Thomas Cox in the early nineteenth century. Cox was a clothier who sold cloth to the East India Company, hence the name. For a time it became a coaching inn when Cox's son Daniel ran daily coaches to London and Bristol. Since its closure in 1964 it has had a variety of uses, and for a time the premises were used for the production of corn dollies. (Photograph by Lockyer).

A Lilywhite postcard of the same inn *c.* 1950.

Four

Slad and Painswick Area

Whilst the Woolpack still flourishes in the small village of Slad, it is surprising that at the time of writing the much larger village (even town) of Painswick possesses only one pub, The Royal Oak, although the Falcon is likely to reopen after refurbishment. Painswick had a number of inns before the last war, including the Bell, Star, White Horse, Golden Heart, Cross Hands, Red Lion and Fleece. The Bell, destroyed by a bomb in 1941 which caused several casualties, was the only local inn to suffer such a fate. The splendid inn sign of the Golden Heart in Tibbiwell Street is still preserved although the inn closed many years ago.

Star Inn, Slad. This superb photograph shows Alfred White who was landlord in 1910 together with his wife Elizabeth and three regulars. Following her husband's death Mrs White continued as licensee for a further twenty years, followed later by Mrs May Edwards whose retirement in 1978 also marked the closure of the inn. Mrs White's granddaughter Mrs Muriel Payne, recalls that a large tablet of Lifebuoy soap was always left beside the stone water trough near the entrance to enable customers to wash their hands before entering. The inn now a private residence has been renamed 'The Buddings'. (Photograph by Lockyer).

Woolpack Inn, Slad. This inn conveniently situated within walking distance of Stroud, was popular long before its comparatively recent association with Laurie Lee and *Cider with Rosie*. It seems likely that the present building (possibly replacing an earlier inn) is contemporary with the church and school, all of which date from *c*. 1830, the Lightpill – Birdlip turnpike having been completed some years earlier. William Daniels, the landlord in 1910, is seen with his family standing on the roadside which apparently lacks a pavement. Note the elaborate signwriting on the gable end and the bird on the chimney pot! (Photograph by Lockyer).

Eagle Inn, Pitchcombe. Situated beside the busy A46, lack of parking facilities no doubt contributed to the demise of the Eagle, an inn which at one time brewed its own ale. On 31 December 1886 Edward Pritchard of Stroud was arrested at the Eagle following the robbery and murder of the young Henry Allen in Lodgemore Lane. He was subsequently hanged at Gloucester. The licensee at this time was Joseph Thomas who was succeeded by Sarah Ann Young whose name appears on this photograph of about 1910 . A more recent proprietor was Victor Hawketts, a well-known local bus driver. (Photograph by Lockyer).

The Golden Hart, Painswick. Unfortunately the photographer considered the left-hand side of Tibbiwell Street more photogenic, but the flamboyant inn sign of the Golden Heart can clearly be seen on the right. The inn provided stabling, possibly in the building with a large entrance opposite.

The Falcon Hotel, Painswick. In prewar days the Falcon as shown in this postcard supplied not only hospitality but also BP petrol, cars for hire and a comprehensive car and lorry repair service. The original inn complete with cockpit and bowling green was built by the Jerninghams, lords of the manor *c.* 1600, but rebuilt in 1711 and tenanted by Elizabeth and William Merritt. The famous bowling green still exists, but happily cock fighting is a thing of the past. Many famous people have patronised the Falcon over the years and it is hoped that its future will be equally rosy.

Ye Royal William, Cranham. The hotel was built in 1830 (during the reign of William IV) to accommodate travellers using the new turnpike between Stroud and Cheltenham. The Royal William with its spacious ballroom and upmarket image, replaced a much inferior hostelry known as 'The Pound of Candles' that was allegedly the haunt of thieves and other undesirables. The photographer when taking this prewar photograph seems quite happy to include the classy motor car in the foreground.

Rising Sun, Randwick. Rather out of place in this section, but is seems a pity to omit this fine photograph showing the pub and the adjacent Methodist chapel, both now sadly closed. Like many other country pubs the Rising Sun was popular with the GIs during the war years, and one can imagine their Jeeps and Chevrolet lorries clogging up the narrow lanes. It is said that a former landlord kept a pet monkey that habitually ran up the tree in front of the pub, presumably causing a nuisance, so the tree had to be removed! Villagers now quench their thirst in the Vine Tree, or further afield at The Carpenter's Arms at Westrip.

Five

Bisley and Hill Villages

The villages around Stroud were well supplied with pubs, and often as in the case of Butterow (included in this section for convenience) two inns both supplying Stroud Ales were situated within a few yards of each other.

Bisley, a small town by eighteenth century standards had as many as ten pubs or beer houses before the collapse of the wool trade in the 1830s. Now only two remain. At Oakridge the Butcher's Arms still thrives, and the Ram at Bussage, the Lamb at Eastcombe and the Old Neigbourhood at Chalford also serve the rapidly increasing population.

Lamb Inn, Butterow. This fascinating old photograph shows a group of tidily dressed women standing outside what would have then been regarded as a predominantly male establishment. Alfred Ind the licensee in 1907 and when the photograph was taken is conspicuous by his absence! Like its neighbour, the Woolpack, the complete lack of parking facilities led to the closure of the Lamb, which is now a private residence. It is interesting to note that the inn was valued in 1924 at £700. (Photograph by Lockyer).

Princess Royal, Butterow. The local gentry may have patronised the Bear or the Prince Albert, but the ordinary folk' might have found Francis Ashenford's humbler tavern more to their liking. Note the impatient customer lurking in the background! This old inn made a pleasant break for walkers from Stroud en route to Rodborough Common, but sadly this is yet another Butterow pub that no longer offers hospitality. (Photograph by Lockyer).

Red Lion, Eastcombe. This substantial Victorian inn built *c.* 1870 which together with two adjoining cottages was valued at £700 in 1917, closed just two years later. The building is still recognisable complete with its stone lion. This animal is said to leave the roof for his dinner when the chapel clock strikes twelve! The landlord at the time of the photograph was Arthur Davis, but Godfrey Davis (his son?) was licensee in 1910 and for at least four subsequent years. (Photograph by Lockyer).

George Inn, Bisley. When this photograph was taken some eighty years ago the George inn was tied to the Nailsworth Brewery, and finally sold West Country ales before its closure in 1969. It has since been converted into a general grocery shop and post office. The photographer was Gerald Drummond who lived at the Chantry and was probably inspired by Fred Major. During the First World War, Gerald joined the Scot's Guards, went to the Western Front and was killed in action shortly before the end of hostilities. (Photograph by Drummond).

Bear Inn, Bisley. One of the oldest inns in the district, certainly dating back to the seventeenth century, The Bear was originally Bisley's Court House and Assembly Room. In 1766 the original Bear inn (just across the road) closed and business was transferred to the present building which for some years incorporated a cobbler's shop. Following a period in the doldrums, the inn gained in popularity after the war when country inns became fashionable with mobile townsfolk. It would need a whole book to do justice to this ancient building with its picturesque façade and alleged secret passages. Suffice to say that it still provides hospitality in a setting unspoilt by pseudo restoration. (Photograph by Drummond).

New Inn, Bisley. This old inn, now trendily renamed 'The Stirrup Cup' may not be as old as the Bear, but is certainly as popular. The Skinner family were licensees for at least forty years during which time they also ran a butcher's shop on the premises and hired out coaches and conveyances. The best known landlord in recent years was Les Restall, a member of another equally well known family.

New Inn, Bisley. This 'advertising card' was actually sent to a friend in Daglingworth by Mrs Skinner in January 1908.

The Bell Inn, Bisley. This excellent Bisley postcard, the work of Fred Major, was posted in 1918, but the photograph would have been taken some years earlier, as the Bell is believed to have closed in 1911. Mr Sherwood, the bearded landlord, is standing on the extreme left, and the central group includes Richard Liddicot who became a gardener at Lypiatt Park. The building is now the HQ of the local British Legion.

Railway Tavern, Brownshill. Surely a misnomer as the railway must be at least a mile away, and many would prefer its original name 'The Barley Mow'. The Stroud Brewery valued the inn at £950 in 1900. This attractive little pub closed some years ago and has since been subjected to some form of renovation. Apparently this work has been abandoned and the building now presents a sorry appearance. (Photograph by Lockyer).

Butcher's Arms, Oakridge. For many years a simple village inn, The Butchers Arms has developed into a pub/restaurant popular with customers from a wide area. Philip Gardiner landlord in the 1960-70 period was an excellent woodworker, his father Fred Gardiner, having been trained in the Gimson tradition. Over a hundred years earlier Paul Gardiner kept the inn and also attended the Methodist Chapel and sang in the choir. Clearly he had no problems in reconciling both spiritual and physical thirst. (Lilywhite postcard *c.* 1950).

The Crown, Waterlane. This attractive little inn closed its doors in 1969, and is now a private residence. The last licensee was Mrs Howkins who from my own recollection was not particularly welcoming to strangers! (Lilywhite postcard).

Nelson Inn, Far Oakridge. This typical country inn has been visited by many of the well-known personalities who have chosen to live in this part of the Cotswolds. During the Second World War period, Max Beerbohm daily walked to the inn to buy cigarettes, and more recently Robert Mawdesley (the first 'Walter Gabriel') made the pub his local. Larry Connors the last landlord before the inn closed in 1969 also farmed the adjacent smallholding. (Lilywhite postcard).

Mechanics Arms, Chalford Hill. The landlord and his wife, posing outside their pub, would hardly recognise the premises today. Now renamed The Old Neighbourhood (although older residents still refer to it as 'The Mechanics') the inn has been greatly extended and is now a popular pub/restaurant. In this nostalgic scene the building on the left is a storehouse, and the left foreground is mainly a chicken run. (Photograph by Lockyer).

Duke of York, Chalford Hill. This early nineteenth-century building derived its name from the former lords of the manor (the Mortimers) who were Dukes of York. The property was originally owned by William Yarnton Mills who also owned the White Hart Inn in Bisley, and several other properties. The two inns were acquired by Albert Crook in 1891 for £905, and he made a good profit when he sold the Duke of York alone to Stroud Brewery four years later for £850. The inn reach its zenith of popularity when it was much frequented by airmen from nearby Aston Down, but finally closed its doors a few years ago and is now a private residence.

Oak Inn, Frampton Mansell. This isolated inn would have derived most of its trade from the bargees using the Thames and Severn Canal, and not surprisingly ceased operations when this section of the waterway closed around 1922. No doubt the landlord, Samuel Elliott had to supplement his income with some more gainful occupation, while Emily, his wife, ran the pub during the day. Emily outlived her husband by some thirty-three years, working on Puck Mill Farm and later, energetically fundraising for the proposed Frampton Mansell Village Hall. Compare the signwriting on the gable with that on the Woolpack Inn on page 42. (Photograph by Lockyer).

Six

Amberley and Minchinhampton

The popularity of the golf courses, commons and countryside in this part of the Cotswolds must account for the number of hotels, inns and guest houses operating earlier this century. The Stroud Brewery's flagship in this region was probably the Amberley Inn which still flourishes, but two of the three Box pubs have long closed, and only The Crown serves Minchinhampton apart from the 'out of town' Old Lodge and Ragged Cot.

The Amberley Inn. Motor traffic is decidedly absent in this early 1900 postcard view. The Amberley Inn was built in 1855 and was extensively altered and modernised some seventy years later. Maurice Gilmore, a popular licensee, took over the inn after the last war, since when it has been a favoured hotel and restaurant. (Wrench Series Postcard).

Black Horse Inn, Amberley. The patriarchal gentleman standing with his wife in the foreground is Henry Walker who would have been licensee around 1910, when the inn was valued at no less that £1,200! In recent years the addition of a conservatory affording a commanding view of the Woodchester valley, and the provision of a wide range of food has made the Black Horse a popular venue. (Photograph by Lockyer).

Box Inn, Box. I have found very little information about the Box Inn apart from the fact that during the summer of 1943 the landlord put down a wooden skittle alley at the back of his house for the benefit of the American GIs who were encamped in large numbers near Minchinhampton. The building was valued at £1,300 in 1900, and became a private house in 1967. The unusual stonework around the doors and windows is of interest. One doorway immediately to the right of the drainpipe has been blocked off, and an old washtub has been placed under the down pipe to collect the water. (Photograph by Lockyer).

Salutation Inn, Minchinhampton. This popular inn known to locals as 'The Sally' closed in the 1960s, and was purchased by F.A. Wall & Sons whose electrical business had previously been higher up Tetbury Street.

Salutation Inn. The characters shown in the previous photograph deserve an enlargement. Their dress and the shiny pavement suggest a cold damp day.

Ram Inn, Minchinhampton. This ancient hostelry has been an inn since late in the seventeenth century, and prior to 1750 was known as 'The Pen and Hand'. Before 1897 The Ram was owned by the Forwood Brewery, and Charles Keen shown in the photograph became landlord *c.* 1906. The inn has recently been converted into a restaurant. (Photograph by Lockyer).

Crown Inn, Minchinhampton. The *Stroud Free Press* of 13 January 1854 had this advertisement: 'CROWN HOTEL MINCHINHAMPTON ONE MILE FROM THE BRIMSCOMBE STATION. PRIVATE APARTMENTS FOR FAMILIES. WITH A DIRECT ACCESS THROUGH THE PARK TO MINCHINHAMPTON COMMON, WHENCE COMMANDING VIEWS ARE OBTAINED OF THE VALE OF BERKELEY, AND THE RIVER SEVERN EXTENDING TO THE FOREST OF DEAN, THE WELSH & MALVERN HILLS ETC. ETC. TERMS MODERATE. SADDLE & POST HORSES, GIGS, FLYS ETC. ETC. FOR HIRE. THE SALUBRITY OF THE SITUATION OF MINCHINHAMPTON IS WELL KNOWN, AND THE FACT STATED BY THE REGISTRAR GENERAL IN HIS REPORT, THAT CHOLERA IS TO BE FOUND LESS FATAL IN PROPORTION TO THE ELEVATION OF THE SITE, WILL GIVE TO THIS BEAUTIFUL LOCALITY AN ADDITIONAL ATTRACTION.' Now the one and only hostelry in the village, the extensive premises are often used for art exhibitions and antique sales. (Photograph by Lockyer).

White Hart, Minchinhampton. Mr S.T.W. Furley stands outside his extremely shabby premises. The upper windows are broken, the rendering is flaking away and a collection of barrels partly obstruct the pavement. Hardly an advertisement for the brewery! The inn closed many years ago and the premises have been converted into shops. (Photograph by Lockyer).

Trumpet Inn, Minchinhampton. The Trumpet Inn appears to have lost its inn sign in this photograph. The licensee in 1907 was Edward Grant who may be the gentleman by the doorway. Ray and Alma Ward took over the inn in 1967, but it closed some years later and is now an antique shop. (Photograph by Lockyer).

Kings Head Inn, Forwood. Although Hannah Hillman is shown as licensee in the photograph, Kelly's Directory indicates that Hannah Workman was landlady between 1910 and 1914, possibly the same person having changed her name on marriage. The main internal feature was a huge pike caught in Woodchester Park lake, displayed in a glass case over the mantlepiece. This was another closure in the 1960s, and the inn is now in private occupation. (Photograph by Lockyer).

Ragged Cot Inn, Minchinhampton. Acquired from Cooks of Tetbury in 1913, the inn was little more than a cottage until enlarged by the Stroud Brewery Co in 1926. It is reputedly haunted by the ghost of a woman who died whilst trying to prevent her landlord husband from carrying out a robbery. In more recent times it was much frequented by airmen from nearby Aston Down and the popular wartime landlord Harry Cox was himself employed as a clerk on the aerodrome. Mrs Cox ran the RAF officer's mess in the pub smoke room. (Photograph by Peckham).

Seven

Selsley and Stonehouse Valley

This section covers Selsley, part of which is more appropriate to the Nailsworth valley, and also Nympsfield and Uley, which strictly should be included with Dursley. There appear to have been fewer closures in this area, particularly in Stonehouse which still retains at least five inns.

Eastington with two pubs is however a far cry from the situation in 1839 when the village, not only had two pubs, but also 23 'beer shops'. The population at the time was 715, giving one beer shop to every 31 inhabitants!

New Inn, Selsley. The closure of many inns by Whitbreads during the late 1960s can perhaps be justified on economic grounds, but the demolition of this homely country inn following its closure in 1967 was little short of vandalism. The ancient building with its snugs and outdoor skittle alley was popular both summer and winter, and the site is now empty, identified only by concrete marker posts. Len Hogg, landlord earlier this century retired to a cottage on the edge of the common, and many years later the writer and his family occupied the same cottage for fifteen years.

New Inn, Selsley. Ernest Cratchley, who was landlord of the inn for thirty-two years up to 1960 is seen intently watching the action on the skittle alley. The children are from left to right, Ivor Lusty, Marjorie Lusty, Vera Cratchley the landlord's daughter, and Mervyn Lusty. The cow's name is not known! It is recalled that the local vicar Revd Habgood could on occasion be found helping to serve pints behind the tiny bar.

Weavers Arms, Middleyard. Tucked away down Greencourt, a small side turning in Middleyard, the Weavers Arms, now a private house, is difficult to locate. In this 1910 photograph the landlord, Arthur Kendall, poses proudly outside his inn with customers, helpers or maybe members of his family. (Photograph by Lockyer).

The Coach and Horses, Ebley. One of several Ebley pubs which included the Lamb, the Malakoff and the Old Crown. The photograph was taken in 1926 when the proprietor may have been A.G. Vick who was certainly there in 1930. This gentleman emphasised the inn's virtues, including the fact that buses stopped at the door, and he also offered 'every attention'! In 1900 the property comprising, inn and five cottages was valued at £1,800.

The Old Castle Inn. The licensee on this postcard is George Fletcher, who kept the inn prior to 1922 before it passed to Edgar Malpass. Mr Fletcher was also a farmer, selling produce locally or at market, and he also hired out wagonettes and other horse-drawn vehicles.

Star Inn, Kings Stanley. The solitary elderly lady standing by the gate in this 1910 photograph is probably the wife of the landlord Charles Fletcher, father of George Fletcher who subsequently took over the Old Castle Inn. This inn has been closed for many years and is now in private occupation. (Photograph by Lockyer).

New Inn, Kings Stanley. Now a private house known as 'The Old New Inn', this solid looking building was delicensed around 1960. The landlord from 1923 was Louis Dangerfield who also operated a bakery business next door, which has expanded considerably in recent years.

Haywardsfield Inn, Ryeford. This inn, now a private house and located by the main A419 at 'Nowhere', was sold together with two brick built pig sties for £525 in 1931. This photograph shows the inn when Gilbert Henry Hathaway was licensee.

This contrasting photograph taken shortly afterwards shows the inn considerably spruced up. The new landlord Percy Selby and his wife also seem to be a cut above their predecessors!

Crown & Anchor Hotel. This handsome building still successfully functioning today, is mentioned in Parish Records as early as 1815. The licensee contemporary with the postcard was W.R. Hopkins a well-known parish councillor who was previously a draper.

Royal Arms, Stonehouse. The history of this rather elaborate building is obscure, but presumably the gentleman standing outside is the landlord George Tocknell. Happily this is another Stonehouse pub that has escaped closure. (Photograph by Lockyer).

Spa Inn, Stonehouse. This old inn possibly dating from the sixteenth century and situated in Oldends Lane, still thrives. This slightly gruesome photograph shows the locals outside the pub proudly displaying their spoils. I assume that the gentleman on the extreme right is the landlord. (Photograph by Lockyer).

Victoria Inn, Eastington. One of Eastington's two remaining inns, the Victoria is thought to date from the 1850s. In this photograph of *c.* 1920 the landlord appears to be wearing riding breeches. A Sgt Crowther was a well-known licensee in post-war years.

Britannia Inn, Eastington. Four locals perhaps including the landlord, Arthur Dowdeswell, pose outside the Britannia in this photograph of *c.* 1920. It is unlikely that they found it necessary to chain their bicycles to the fence! This is yet another inn closed in the 1960s to revert to private occupation.

The Britannia's last inn sign following the merger between the Stroud and Cheltenham & Hereford Breweries.

Kings Head Hotel, Eastington. Formerly a large private house The Kings Head was probably first licensed early in Victoria's reign, there was certainly a licensee Samuel West there in 1859. The Stroud Brewery acquired the premises from the Tetbury New Brewery in 1913 and it is now a free house. In 1897 Charles Hooper a wealthy industrialist and temperance advocate erected a drinking fountain (seen on the right of the photograph) in front of the Kings Head so that no one need be driven to alcohol by thirst. Waterless for decades, it now serves only as a rather attractive signpost. (Photograph by Lockyer).

Inn sign by Mike Hawkes.

Rose & Crown Inn, Nympsfield. This old inn, one of five such in earlier times, may have been originally known as 'The Ducie Arms'. Popular in Edwardian times, an advertisement in Symonds 1907 directory reads thus: 'FIRST CLASS HOUSE FOR BOARDING RESIDENTS IN THE MOST PICTURESQUE PART OF GLOUCESTERSHIRE. EXCELLENT CATERING AND CAPITAL ACCOMMODATION FOR VISITORS, PICNIC PARTIES, CYCLISTS ETC. AN IDEAL SPOT TO SPEND A WEEKEND. GOOD STABLING. ROWLAND J. FORD PROP.' The same hospitality with probably a much more varied menu is still available today 90 years later. (Lilywhite postcard *c.* 1960).

Old Crown Inn, Uley. Often called the 'Top Crown' to distinguish it from the 'Lower Crown' further down the street even though the latter closed many years ago. This inn was well placed to do a roaring trade when Uley Feast took place on the green in the foreground, in prewar days. A special room was provided where women and children could relax while their men folk had a drink. (Lilywhite postcard *c.* 1960).

Eight
Woodchester and Nailsworth

There was no shortage of pubs in the populous Nailsworth valley, and in some places they were literally 'cheek by jowl'. The Stroud Brewery however did not have the same monopoly in Nailsworth as elsewhere, as the local brewery was acquired by their Cheltenham competitors in 1908.

The Old Fleece Inn, Woodchester. Some readers will remember the days when Ben Ford ran the pub and on occasions arrived on the forecourt splendidly attired and driving a carriage and four. Things were not always so good and in 1938 the landlady in a letter to the Brewery complained bitterly about the dreadful state of the building. 'This house really is falling to pieces, rain not only coming in on the beds but all over the house, the dirty walls are alarming one only feels they are eating dirt to look at them. I have even had to put curtains up on the stairs to try and hide holes in the walls. The bedroom floors are giving way and the kitchen – we would get unto trouble if we tried to keep pigs in it.' Let's hope the brewery acted speedily to put matters right, but there is little likelihood of today's visitors finding anything so seriously amiss!

The Ram Inn, Woodchester. The present Ram Inn looks considerably more inviting than the austere premises presided over by Henry Dowling in 1910. Basil Latham was licensee for many years before and after the last war. (Photograph by Lockyer).

Crown Inn, Inchbrook. The present inn has changed considerably since the photograph was taken c. 1910. It was here in the early 1940s whilst working as a junior clerk at Newman Henders that I sampled my first glass of beer before returning unsteadily to my duties! The 1928 *Gloucestershire Guide* refers to the Crown as a 'real old fashioned inn delightfully situated offering good fare and homely comfort'. (Photograph by Lockyer).

Plough Inn, Woodchester. This appears to be the inn at Little Britain next to Workman's Sawmills which closed in the 1920s and has since been demolished. The landlady looks spruce but the building appears to have suffered some subsidence. Note the 'jug and bottle' department discreetly located at the side of the inn. (Photograph by Lockyer).

Ten Bells, Frogmarsh. This fine building may once have served as the mill owner's house for nearby Frogmarsh Mill, and it is once more privately occupied. Sophie Latham the licensee around 1910 was probably related to Basil Latham who managed the Ram Inn a generation later. (Photograph by Lockyer).

Jovial Forester, Forest Green. Forest Green had no shortage of inns, The Star, The Upper Star and The Jovial Forester were all within a stones throw of each other, whilst The Rock and Fountain was just at the top of Star Hill. Today only 'The Foresters' survives as a pub. Presumably licensee Sidney Smith was busy elsewhere when his wife and daughter posed for the photograph. (Photograph by Lockyer).

Star Inn, Forest Green. Situated within a few yards of the Jovial Forester, The Star was recorded in 1839, and the building is probably even earlier. The landlord in 1859 was E. Hewley, but the name of the licensee in the photograph is not known. The inn closed in the 1960s and is now a private residence. (Photograph by Lockyer).

The Upper Star, Forest Green. Now called Star Cottage, this little inn was delicensed *c.* 1922, the Stroud Brewery having acquired it from the Tetbury New Brewery in 1913. The property incorporating dwelling house, stable, two store houses, cart shed, pig sties and 1½ acres of land was sold to William Haines, a poultry farmer for £500 in 1924.

Rising Sun Inn, Shortwood. Originally situated at the rear of Nodes Cottages, the inn was nicknamed the 'Rotten Rail' on account of the rickety hand rail over a plank bridge which resulted in unsteady patrons falling into the stream. The Rising Sun moved to its present site around 1870, and now following its closure, presents a rather dilapidated spectacle. (Photograph by Lockyer).

Clothiers Arms, Nailsworth. The ornate bracket and inn sign was probably the outstanding feature, but the building itself, dating prior to 1820 was listed as of architectural interest. In Victorian times The Clothiers was the terminus for horse buses running between Stroud and Nailsworth. Originally a Godsell's pub it was acquired by Stroud Brewery in 1928, closed forty years later, and demolished shortly afterwards.

Red Lion, Nailsworth. This humble little inn at the foot of Butcher's Hill Lane was the location of the original Nailsworth Urban District Council office before the authority moved to George Street in 1934. The notice in the pub window of this 1904 postcard advertises a 'Musical Evening'. The inn is believed to have closed around 1910.

George Hotel, Nailsworth. The George is shown shortly after its extensive renovation and modernisation in the early 1950s. Following its comparatively recent closure it was threatened with demolition, but now plans are in hand to give a new commercial life to the premises. (Photograph by Peckham).

The George in1910 presented a rather more homely appearance. It was an important coaching and posting house in Victorian times for coaches bound for Bristol, Birmingham and Bath and later was a terminus for horse buses linking the town with Stroud.

Nags Head Inn, Dunkirk. Situated beside the A46 less than a mile from Nailsworth, the Nags Head was in direct competition with the Crown at Inchbrook and the Kings Head which occupied the same terraced block of property. The former Kings Head still remains, but the Nags Head which also closed many years ago has been demolished to provide space for a car sales forecourt. (Photograph by Lockyer).

White Hart Inn, Downend Horsley. This inn was recorded in 1798, but the building must be much earlier. William and Ellen Harvey were licensees early this century before moving to the Bell and Castle. William was injured losing an eye when a pop bottle exploded in his face, and a subsequent landlord Cmdr. Jarvis died in an air crash. Two former customers Charlie Holborow and his son, were noted for smoking churchwarden pipes and causing a fug in the tiny bar. The inn is believed to have closed in the 1960s and is now privately owned.

Bell & Castle, Horsley. This inn is obviously much earlier than its recorded date of 1870. William and Helen Harvey who were licensees for some thirty years kept cows, pigs and chickens on an adjacent smallholding selling milk, butter and eggs as a sideline. Two black horses provided transport and these were often in demand for funerals. William also owned the football field where the players changed in a cowshed. The inn has now been extended and includes a popular restaurant. (Lilywhite postcard).

George Inn, Newmarket. The inn which opened in 1820 as The New Inn, originally comprised three cottages. It has recently been opened up internally and provides an attractive small restaurant area. The landlord in this photograph of *c.* 1910 was Henry Nicholls. (Photograph by Lockyer).

Black Horse Inn, Horsley. The present building appears to have been built as a roadside inn, and cannot date back much earlier than 1888, when it was known to be a Stroud Brewery property. The Tiltups Inn which apparently occupied the same site was however recorded as far back as 1769. Recently the inn situated at Tiltups End, a mile or so out of Nailsworth on the A46 has been rather confusingly renamed the Tipputs Inn.

Cross Inn, Avening. Although recorded as an inn in 1856, when James Sharp was the landlord, the building must be centuries earlier. The Cross has been extensively altered in recent years, but contains interesting features including a painting of a former regular who allegedly always slept in a chair, never a bed.

Bell Inn, Avening. A notice inside the pub indicates that the inn together with three cottages and half an acre of land was sold in 1866. Many years later it was acquired by the Stroud Brewery together with an orchard known as Brassingtons. The Bell which has recently reopened stands at the bottom of New Inn Lane, and the former New Inn now renamed Glebe House can be found a little higher up.

Nine
Dursley, Wotton and Severnside

In 1928 the Stroud Brewery owned approximately thirty public houses and hotels in this area including no less that ten in Wotton-under-Edge. The Kingshill Inn in Dursley was probably the Stroud Brewery's most ambitions building project in pre-Second World War days.

Off Licence, Saul. Stonebree Cottage served as Saul's Off Licence for decades and customers used a small hatch at the rear of the premises. When this photograph was taken *c.* 1930 the license was held by John Duncan Victor Willy Harris, who was also a baker, unofficial bookmaker and leading member of the Parish Council. Following his death the license was transferred to John's son-in-law and daughter Tom and Ruth Barham and it remained in the family for a further fifty years.

Drover's Arms, Cambridge. The private house standing beside the A38 just outside the village of Cambridge bears scant resemblance to the inn in the photograph. The Stroud Brewery became the owners in 1888 and Charles Pegler was licensee when the photograph was taken c. 1910. The inn was still operating in 1959 when a motorist was threatened with court action for failing to pay damages of £6 10s 0d after hitting a projecting ornamental lamp! (Photograph by Lockyer).

Darrell Arms, Framilode. This ornate mock Tudor building superseded The Passage House Inn where licensee Thomas Cullis had a coal yard and also operated the ferry whilst his wife provided refreshment and accommodation at the inn. The inn was owned by the Darrell family who often supported social and sporting activities in the village, and the line up of open tourers in the photograph suggests that this was one of their regular pub visits! The inn closed recently and is now privately owned.

Three Horseshoes, Frampton-on-Severn. Now owned by Whitbreads, this inn, the smaller of the two remaining in the village is popular with both visitors and locals. This 1911 postcard showing four men standing rather stiffly outside the premises indicates that beer, ale, porter and cider are available but presumably no wines or spirits.

Ship Inn, Framilode. This canalside inn appears to date from early last century and would have been frequented by the bargees and canal workers. The canal trade declined but Framilode with its tea gardens became popular with day trippers some of whom preferred more potent refreshment. Harry Rudge the licensee when this photograph was taken *c.* 1910 may have been one of the landlords who had a small coal business and also kept pigs which were killed and salted in the cellar. Nowadays there are no tea gardens but the Ship still provides hospitality. (Photograph by Lockyer).

Bell Inn, Arlingham. The Bell is not included in the Stroud Brewery's 1928 pub list, so no doubt this photograph was taken some time later. It closed many years ago, was demolished and the site now provides access to the new Bell Orchard development.

Red Lion, Arlingham. Nowadays the only inn left in the village. The Red Lion was formerly a Godsells pub so this photograph is presumably post 1928 although it appears to be earlier. The inn, now a free house still retains its rustic character.

George Inn, Cambridge. Strategically situated on the A38 this much enlarged inn provides food and drink to many a weary traveller. Formerly a leasehold property of the Stroud Brewery it is now owned by Whitbreads.

Railway Inn, Cam. The smart young couple posing by their motor car contrast sharply with the group of becapped regulars in the background. Joseph Ireland the landlord, when this mid 1930s photograph was taken, may be the man standing in the doorway. The railway has gone, but happily the inn still survives.

Kingshill Inn, Dursley. Built as an integral part of the ambitious Kingshill development this handsome building opened the day after the outbreak of the last war. The first licensee was Mr L.W. Collins who had previously been an architect and surveyor to the local council. Now owned by Wadworths, with painted brickwork, fancy lanterns and a non-matching extension, the inn rather lacks the pristine appearance seen in the photograph.

Bell & Castle Inn, Dursley. Tom Vigus and his daughter stand proudly outside their 'family and commercial hotel' in Parsonage Street. The cyclist, possibly a prospective client, waits to one side having seen the CTC plaque beside the entrance. The building was demolished some years ago to make way for extensive road alterations. (Photograph by Lockyer).

Crown Inn, Dursley. Charles Owen the licensee for several years prior to 1914 is seen here with his wife and daughter. Presumably the building was in some disrepair when sold by Stroud Brewery for £270 in 1939. In recent years it became a wine bar called 'The Inn Place' but is again empty. The decorative semi-circular window now contains clear glass but the attractive corner sections remain. (Photograph by Lockyer).

Apple Tree Inn, Wotton-under-Edge. The pub appears to have the decorators in and not before time judging from its somewhat shabby appearance. The landlord Charles Mace, who is presumably in the photograph sold Royal Daylight Lamp Oil as a side line. The inn has been a private dwelling since 1959. (Photograph by Lockyer).

Swan Hotel, Wotton-under-Edge. Wotton's premier hotel for many years. The Swan is now largely a bistro and coffee bar. During Victorian times the hotel was a commercial and posting house, an excise office and the centre for coaches linking Wotton with neighbouring towns and the local railway station at Charfield.

New Inn, Kingswood. The New Inn closed many years ago and has been converted into a desirable residence, recently offered for sale at £169,000. The Stroud Brewery valued the premises at £1,000 in 1900! The building allegedly dates back to the fifteenth century and was refronted in the eighteenth century. Some of the original pub glass is still preserved. (Photograph by Lockyer).

Bell Inn, Berkeley Heath. A principal coaching inn and changing post for nearly 200 years this inn, then known as The Swan dates from 1728. Renamed The Bell in 1751 it became Stroud Brewery property in 1909 costing £2,525. It was subsequently sold with sixty-eight acres to Mr C.H. Barber, renamed the Chestnuts and following his death the license was relinquished. A notable visitor was Charles Dickens who dined at the inn en route to Tewkesbury in 1837. The property is now appropriately called Pickwick Farm. (Photograph by Lockyer).

George Inn, Berkeley. This photograph was taken before 1914 when W. Stump was the licensee. The inn lasted until 1990 and has recently become a retail outlet for Broadmark Furniture. The building has been roughcast but the inn sign and Brewery plaque remain. (Photograph by Lockyer).

Berkeley Vale Hotel, Stone. Now called the Berkeley Vale Inn, this Victorian coaching inn has been greatly altered in recent years, and the stables have been converted into a skittle alley. The inn has had a chequered history and for a time became a gentlemen's rest home, before resuming its normal usage as Stone's one and only pub. (Photograph by Adams c. 1950).

Ten

Tetbury and Malmesbury

The Stroud Brewery extended its operations significantly during the periods just before and after the First World War. The breweries of N & W Cook of Tetbury, and Luce of Malmesbury, were acquired during 1912/13, and these were followed by Duck & Co of Malmesbury and Butler's Marlborough brewery in 1920. As a result a large proportion of the public houses in these towns came under Stroud Brewery ownership although a number were subsequently sold off.

Royal Oak, Leighterton. This inn was one of a number of properties sold by Huntleys of nearby Boxwell Court in 1903, when it came into Stroud Brewery ownership. During the First World War it served as the local for the Australian airmen stationed nearby, several of whom lost their lives during training. Relatives of these airmen still visit Leighterton and mementoes of those days are displayed in the Royal Oak which is now a free house. (Photograph by Lockyer).

New Inn, Knockdown. This fascinating photograph showing some sort of building work in progress hardly suggests a genteel establishment. For many years the building served as a farmhouse and blacksmith's shop before becoming a public house. The inn was renamed the Holford Arms in recent years to commemorate the Westonbirt squire who was responsible for the famous arboretum. (Photograph by Lockyer).

(Enlargement). Lockyer always liked to include people in his photographs, and no doubt the workmen were quite happy to take a short break.

Greyhound Hotel, Tetbury. Largely unchanged externally but altered within to suit the current fashion, the Greyhound is far removed from the simple hostelry shown in the photograph. The arched entrance below the projecting lantern would presumably have served both man and beast.

Crown Inn, Tetbury. Formerly the property of the Romney family the Crown dates back to at least 1594. Originally known as the Angel it was renamed The Crown *c.* 1900 to avoid confusion with another 'Angel' in the town. The building was extensively 'improved' in the seventeenth century and recent alterations have provided the inn with a popular restaurant area. (Photograph by Lockyer).

Bell Inn, Tetbury. Situated in New Church Street, the former Bell has lost its ornate portal and is now divided into flats. George Beale was the licensee when this photograph was taken shortly after the inn came into Stroud Brewery ownership in about 1913. The date of closure is unclear but was prior to 1949. (Photograph by Lockyer).

Eight Bells Inn, Tetbury. This comparatively modern postcard shows the inn following its acquisition by Whitbreads. With its distinctive timber framed gables jettied over the pavement, the building could date back to the Tudor period. Its early history is obscure but an unfortunate landlord met his death in the 1890s by falling into a well on the premises. Since its closure in the 1970s the premises have had varied usage and currently house a picture framing business.

Plough Inn, Tetbury. The pub looks Victorian but may be much older, the elevated inn sign ensures that no one can doubt its ownership. The mounted soldiers suggest that the postcard is of First World War vintage. The Plough is now serving as a licensed restaurant.

Ormonds Head Hotel, Tetbury. The names comes from the Second Duke of Ormonde who distinguished himself in the service of William III in Ireland, but subsequently became a Jacobite supporter. Originally the building had twin gables facing the street but these were replaced by the present façade in 1902. At one time the inn was known as the Blue House, later The Lamb and Flag and nowadays it is merely an off-licence still bearing the current name 'The Gentle Gardener'. (Cotswold Publishing Co Postcard).

Green Dragon, Malmesbury. Situated near the Market Cross, this fifteenth-century building originally had a projecting arcade to shelter market traders. Following its closure and sale in 1922 it became a shop owned by a Miss Long, but was converted to a private dwelling in 1957. The premises are now in use as a licensed restaurant. (Photograph by Lockyer).

Railway Hotel, Malmesbury. Subsequently renamed 'The Flying Monk' this solid looking building closed and was demolished in 1985. The site is now occupied by a large supermarket. (Photograph by Lockyer).

George Hotel, Malmesbury. Formerly an important coaching inn, this substantial eighteenth century building extended back to Cross Hayes. Delicensed in 1978 the premises are now used as a veterinary hospital. The posters on the scaffolding relate to a sale of cattle at Braydon, a religious meeting and a performance of Stainer's Crucifixion in the abbey of 13 May 1913. (Photograph by Lockyer).

Castle Inn, Malmesbury. Originally 'The Weavers Arms', The Castle was sold in 1961 for £1,100 and is now a private residence. The building was used as an inn in the eighteenth century and later rented for eight guineas a year by James Pratt who found it necessary to apply for parish relief in 1901. The last landlord prior to closure was Alan Adams. (Photograph by Lockyer).

Barley Mow, Malmesbury. Following its closure in 1921 the property was sold for £150 to Mr F. Salter, the landlord, for residential use. The interior has since been extensively altered for use as a dental surgery. (Photograph by Lockyer).

Kings Arms, Malmesbury. The top hatted landlord on this postcard may be Henry Jones who was proprietor for some years after 1899. Over 300 years old and one of the principal inns in the town, The Kings Arms served as a commercial inn and posting house, wine and spirit supplier and Inland Revenue office. Mrs Mary Jones was licensee in 1880 when an omnibus met every train to collect hotel guests.

Duke of York, Malmesbury. Some real country characters probably including Edward Henry Hemming the proprietor pose for Lockyer outside this eighteenth century building. The small sign at the end of the building states 'Governess Cart, Pony Trap and Cart for hire'. The building was demolished some years ago. (Photograph by Lockyer).

Duke of York, Malmesbury. This modern replacement would seem to have more in common with Scandinavia than Wiltshire! (Photograph by B. Merrett).

Plough Inn, Malmesbury. George Kane looks the epitome of the landlord cum farmer outside this humble pub near Turtle Bridge. Arthur Slade was the last licensee before the inn closed in 1970, subsequently to be converted into two private properties. (Photograph by Lockyer).

Plough Inn. Road frontage.

Rattlebones Inn, Sherston. The present popular pub/restaurant has altered considerably since this photograph was taken. Named after a warrior whose exploits are legendary, this inn was probably built as a guest house by the local monks in medieval times. The village pump has disappeared along with that part of the building behind the posters. Some older residents recall the day when one risked getting covered in 'hoss muck' on entering.

Rattlebones Inn Sign.

Rose & Crown Inn, Brokenborough. Surely the archetypal village inn judging by this superb 1950 photograph. Today although still recognisable, the old building hides a large restaurant which together with spacious car park and beer garden offers all that the public now expect. I have been unable to ascertain its age or history but the inn was owned by N. and W. Cook of Tetbury until 1913 when it became Stroud Brewery property. The licensee shown in the photograph was William C. Brastock. (Photograph by Peckham).

Angel Inn, Sherston. The Angel appears to need more than a little T.L.C. judging by this 1910 photograph. A plaque on the wall relating to Winifred Goodcheap alias Cowley gives the date 1648, so the building must be well over 300 years old. The inn closed around 1994 and has been converted to offices but 'The Angel' remains! A former licensee was Bristol Rovers footballer George Petherbridge. (Photograph by Lockyer).

Old Royal Ship, Luckington. Still a popular village pub 'The Ship' specialises in food and wines. Apart from a single storey extension in front, the building it largely unaltered, but the walled garden has been removed for car parking. The origin of the name is obscure, possibly ship's timbers were used in its construction. Before the neighbouring Bell Inn closed, it was preferred by some of the locals who referred to 'The Ship' as the 'farmers pub'! (Photograph by Lockyer).

Red Lion, Minety. Strategically sited so close to Minety station that passing trains shook the building, the Old Red Lion was owned by Stroud Brewery in 1888, if not earlier. A former landlord, possibly Jonathan Reed in the photograph, rebuilt the bar so high that he could hardly see over it. When he left in 1926, the then landlord George Griffith was allowed the sum of £42 for his chattels which included eight spittoons, stuffed bantam cock, grandfather clock and sixty-eight pictures. The property is now called Forli Acres (Former Old Red Lion Inn). (Photograph by Lockyer).

Bell Inn, Sherston. Alfred Rice pictured with his son was licensee of this old hostelry not long before the building with the adjoining blacksmith's shop was sold in 1921 for £275. Situated in the High Street near the church, the Bell is now a private house. (Photograph by Lockyer).

Vine Tree Inn, Norton. No longer a simple village pub, The Vine Tree has been roughcast, painted cream with green shutters and would not look out of place in Tuscany. I doubt that Mr Williams (?) and his little family seen here would feel at home there now! (Photograph by Lockyer).

Radnor Arms, Corston. Relatively little outward change here, although the slated section of the mansard roof has been replaced with stone titles. The name derives from the Radnor family whose country seat was in Wiltshire. Sarah Kane the landlady is presumably the woman standing on the right. Was she the mother of George Kane landlord of The Plough in Malmesbury? (Photograph by Lockyer).

Horse & Groom, Charlton. One of the impressive looking ladies in this photograph is the landlady Florence White. The photograph was taken shortly after the inn became the property of the Stroud Brewery as pencil marks on the photograph above the porch indicate the proposed position of the new inn sign.

Enlargement.

Plough Inn, Crudwell. This ancient inn may originally have been a farm house judging by the adjoining barn which has been converted into an attractive restaurant area. A curving driveway between pretty gardens now leads to the car park situated well behind the pub. (Photograph by Adams).

Cat & Custard Pot, Shipton Moyne. Originally a beer house, the premises have been extended since this photograph was taken to include the adjacent cottage. The proposed name 'The Escourt Arms' failed to win the approval of the local squire and the alternative 'Cat & Custard Pot' derives from the novel *Handley Cross* by Surtees, a Stroud Brewery director having recently read the book. Now a popular pub restaurant the license has been held by the same family for 125 years. (Photograph by W. Dennis Moss).

Lion Inn, Yatton Keynell. This fine old building is still quite recognisable, but ceased to be an inn over twenty years ago. It was originally a toll house and the toll board can still be seen in the neighbouring Bell Inn.

Eleven

Gloucester and Cheltenham

A century ago the city of Gloucester possessed 179 inns, taverns and hotels of which at least 21 were in Westgate Street. Ten of these were owned by the Stroud Brewery Co in 1888, but forty years later this number had increased to sixty. During the same period the Brewery's representation in Cheltenham increased from four to twenty-six. Whether Lockyer photographed them all is not known, but out of the twenty included here only five are still functioning as pubs.

New Inn, Tuffley. This former Godsells Inn was acquired by the Stroud Brewery in 1928, demolished after the last war and replaced by the present Fox and Elm.

LLANTHONY CORN MILL,

THE DOCKS, GLOUCESTER.

BRUTON, KNOWLES, & PRIDAY

HAVE RECEIVED INSTRUCTIONS

TO OFFER FOR SALE BY AUCTION,

AT THE NEW INN HOTEL, GLOUCESTER,

ON SATURDAY, DECEMBER 19, 1896,

At 2 for 3 o'clock in the Afternoon, unless previously Sold by Private Contract,

THE LEASE OF

LLANTHONY CORN MILL

For 30 years from the day of completion of the purchase.

The Property comprises a newly and substantially erected Mill, fitted with the following Machinery :—

On the Ground Floor—Gas Engine, by Fielding & Platt, 14-horse-power nominal, working to 34-horse-power, and capable of driving the whole Mill; Stone Hurstings for two pairs of stones.

On the First Floor—Two pairs of stones.

On this Floor there is a small Office.

On the Second Floor—Bolter, Bean Splitter, by Richmond & Chandler, Oat Roll, by Beyer, of Paris, and Gardner's Rapid Mixer, to work by hand or power.

Above is the Bin Floor, with Staging and Hoist.

The Ground and First Floors are each 40ft. × 33ft. 6in.

It is held on Lease from the Stroud Brewery Company, Limited, who have agreed to grant a new Lease to the Purchaser for 30 years, at an annual ground rent of £30. The Machinery will become the absolute property of the Purchaser, subject only to the stipulation that on the termination of the Lease the Stroud Brewery Company may, by giving one month's notice, purchase it by valuation in the usual way.

The Mill occupies an exceptionally good situation, close to the Gloucester Docks, and with a Railway Siding along the front of it.

Further particulars may be had of Messrs. LITTLE & MILLS, Solicitors, Stroud; or of the Auctioneers, Albion Chambers, Gloucester.

Llanthony Corn Mill. Particulars of leasehold property dated 1896.

Black Dog Inn, Gloucester. Black Dog Way is the only reminder that this inn suffered demolition when a section of inner relief road was constructed. It seems likely that the building in the photograph replaced an earlier Black Dog that was in existence in 1705, when widow Winston the licensee was in trouble for having 'suffered tippling on Ye Lords Day'. The building was purchased by Stroud Brewery in 1909 for the then considerable sum of £4,800 and was finally demolished in 1967, when the carved teak-wood dog was carefully removed. This animal, currently, in three sections, awaits restoration in the local museum.

Royal Oak, Hucclecote. As a licensee, Mr E. Smith, is recorded in 1859 it can be concluded that the original Royal Oak dates well back into the nineteenth century. In the 1920s the pub had its own bowling green and club but by 1957 the premises were considered inadequate and Sunnybank the house next door, became the new Royal Oak. The old building was demolished and the site used for car parking.

Fleece Hotel, Wotton, Gloucester. Situated on the Cheltenham Road at Wotton, this rather sombre hotel was demolished a few years ago. It was certainly operating prior to 1859 when Joseph Seabright was the landlord. (Photograph by Lockyer).

Robinswood Inn, Matson. The Stroud Brewery were justly proud of The Robinswood Inn which opened in June 1956, but the only photograph I have shows the rather spartan interior. The rooms are now carpeted and ceiling spotlights have replaced the chandeliers. (Photograph by Peckham).

Anchor Inn, Gloucester. Most of Sweetbriar Street, including the Anchor Inn was demolished some time after 1957, when the pub was sold to the County Borough of Gloucester for £1,350. The inn was first recorded in 1857 so it lasted a little over 100 years. (Photograph by Lockyer).

Theatre Vaults, Westgate Street. Formerly a Godsell's inn as clearly indicated on the postcard, the premises were sited next to the Opera House which subsequently became the Theatre Royal. First recorded in 1891 the inn closed some time after 1957 and the building is currently empty. What remains of the Theatre Royal if anything, is incorporated in the Poundstretcher Store. (Taylor Gloucester Postcard).

Shakespeare Inn, Northgate Street, Gloucester. First recorded in 1820, the Shakespeare Inn was valued at £2,222 in 1900, and in a contemporary advertisement was classed as 'homely and comfortable'. The inn was rebuilt in 1856, extended sometime after this photograph was taken and finally closed *c.* 1959. The premises were last occupied by a firm of estate agents. (Photograph by Lockyer).

Crown Hotel, Gloucester. For over a century this substantial building stood at the corner of Clarence Street and Market Parade. Originally called The Railway Inn it was strategically situated at the business end of Gloucester market and lost much trade when the market was resited. Note the Boodle's Teeth advert on the extreme left of the photograph, no doubt offering 'painless dentistry'! (Photograph by Lockyer).

Worcester Arms, Gloucester. The solitary landlady stands outside what can hardly be described as a salubrious inn! This building including most of Park Street was demolished some years after the last war. (Photograph by Lockyer).

Queens Head Inn, Gloucester. Still standing in what remains of St Catherine Street, the former Queens Head now houses a car accessory firm and presents a rather forlorn appearance. When this photograph was taken *c.* 1930 the inn was the headquarters of the Robert Raikes Lodge and the proprietor was Arthur Waterhouse. The older building extreme right together with the attractive street lamp has disappeared.

Northgate Street, Gloucester. This postcard of *c.* 1910 has been included as it shows the position of The Black Dog Inn, centre right. The Northgate Hotel is on the extreme left and nearer the Cross was The Northgate Wine Vaults later called The Northend Vaults, also owned by the Stroud Brewery Co.

Avenue Hotel, Gloucester. Standing at the corner of Tuffley Avenue, this substantial building was valued at £3,275 in 1900. The proprietor in 1930 was W. Scanlan when the hotel was the HQ of Gloucester Old Boys and offered 'billiards and a fine bowling alley'. (Photograph by Lockyer).

Britannia Inn, Gloucester. A victim of the Lower Westgate Street development, the Britannia was probably demolished twenty or more years ago. The licensee pictured is Sid Smart the well known Rugby footballer. The inn contained a display of International County and City caps and other trophies awarded to Mr Smart during his sporting career.

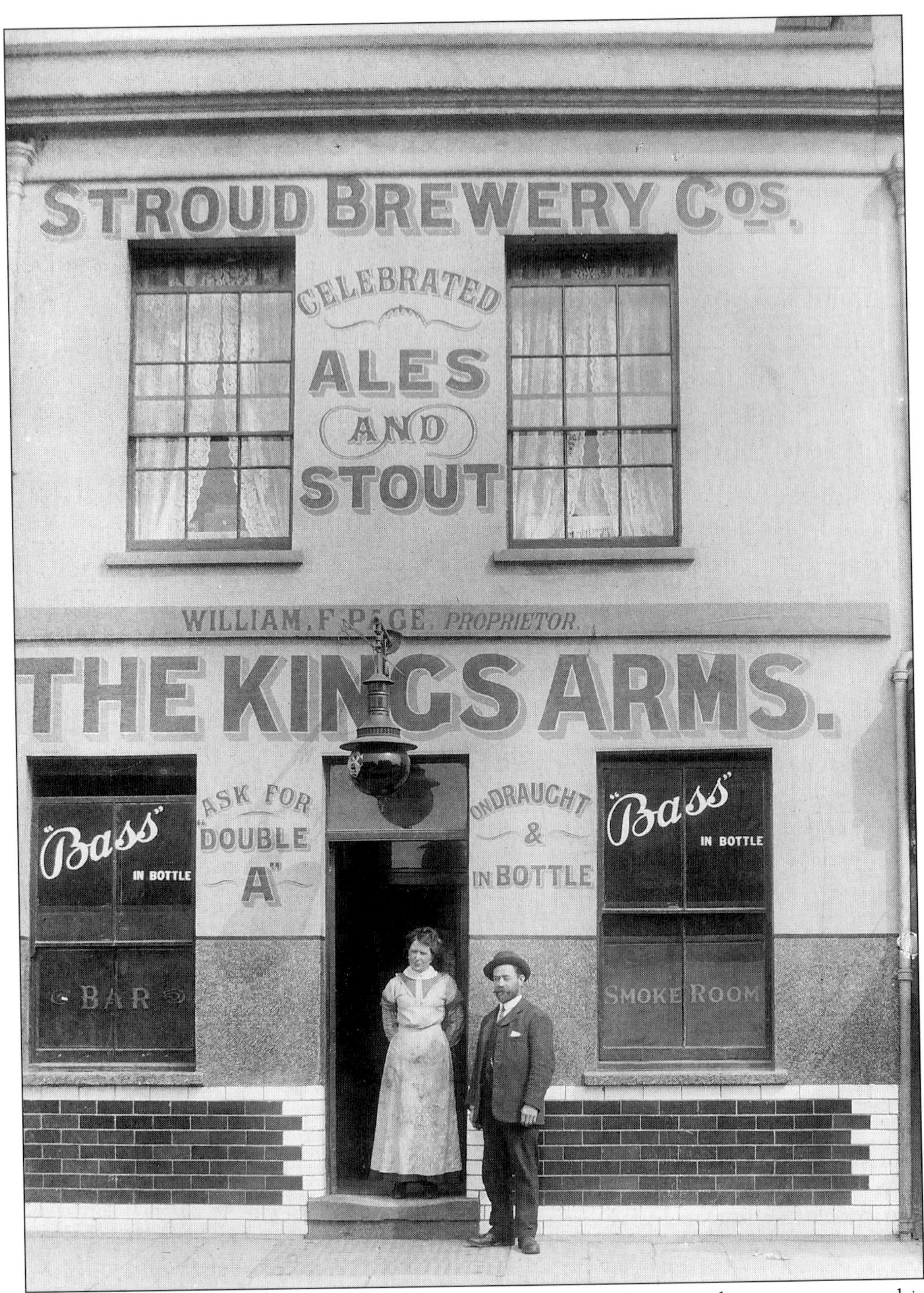

Kings Arms, Cheltenham. One of two Cheltenham inns bearing the same name, this photograph shows The Kings Arms in Clare Terrace, Bath Road. William F. Page the proprietor, and presumably his wife, pose outside their smart premises. Since its closure the inn have been converted into a shop and is now occupied by Pams Pantry. (Photograph by Lockyer).

Wiltshire Brewery, Cheltenham. Situated in Hewlett Place, the pub's unusual name suggests that beer was formerly brewed on the premises, and in fact the property was described in 1906 as brewhouse, wash house, etc. Mr F.J. Cole is the licensee shown in the photograph. Walter Robins his successor in 1930 offered 'an attractive cosy inn with a pretty lawn and garden' (round the back presumably!) Basically unchanged but lacking the signwriter's artwork and ornamental lantern, the premises are now the local RAOB headquarters. (Photograph by Lockyer).

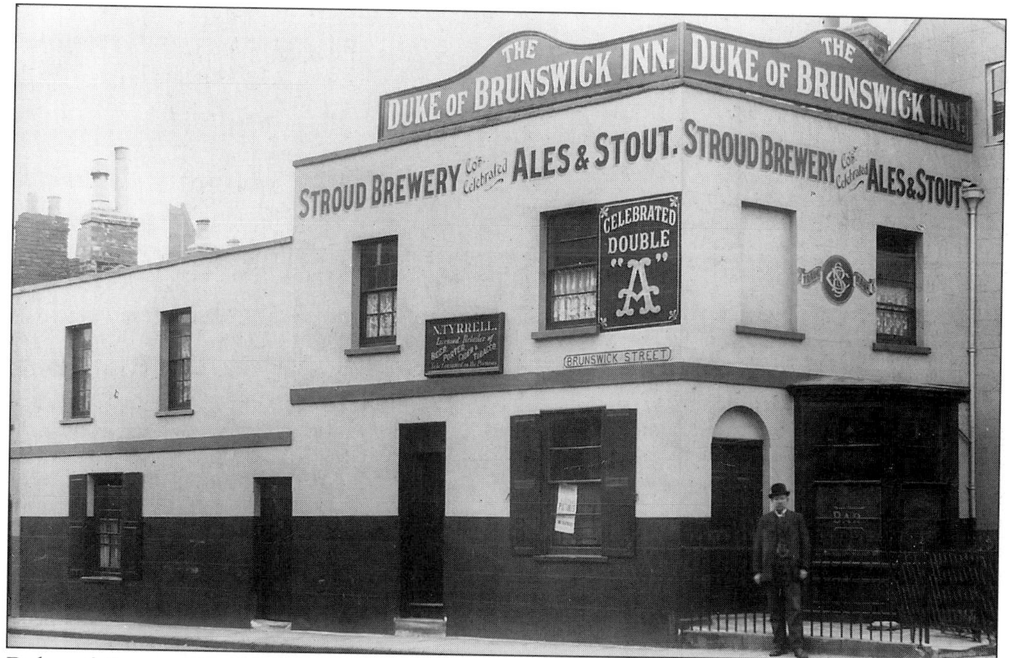

Duke of Brunswick, Cheltenham. Named in honour of the father of Queen Caroline, this smartly decorated building was the responsibility of Mr N. Tyrell in 1912. Following its closure the main building has been converted into a launderette, and the section on the left of the photograph is now a bakery. (Photograph by Lockyer).

Kings Head Hotel, Cheltenham. The fact that the hotel has four 'blind' windows suggests that the building predates the window tax era, but this may be merely an architectural device to preserve symmetry. Demolished some twenty years ago, No. 340 High Street is now occupied by a nondescript building currently in use as a furniture store. (Photograph by Lockyer).

Kings Arms, Cheltenham. Situated in Gloucester Road, the Kings Arms had recently benefitted from the attentions of the Stroud Brewery signwriters when this photograph was taken. Nowadays the artwork and ornamental lantern are missing but the premises still function as a pub. (Photograph by Lockyer).

Twelve

Forest of Dean and Beyond

This final section covers a wide area and shows only a very limited number of the more far flung Stroud Brewery establishments. Locating these old pubs and observing the changes and developments that have affected them has proved quite a fascinating exercise.

New Inn, Whitecroft, Lydney. This photograph is brought to life by the four fascinating characters in the foreground, not forgetting the two dogs. Notice also the well on the left and the apparently damaged trap on the right of the picture. The inn was owned by the Stroud Brewery in 1888 but following closure many years ago is now a smart residence called Kestrel Cottage. (Photograph by Lockyer).

Tump House Inn, Furness Bottom, Blakeney. As so often in Lockyer's photographs, the tidiness of the womenfolk contrasts with the workaday appearance of the men. The pub looks spic and span in its rustic setting and happily, although now a private house, looks much the same today. James Reeves, who may be in the photograph, was landlord *c.* 1910. (Photograph by Lockyer).

White Hart Inn, Broadoak, Newnham. Sadly progress has overtaken The White Hart, an inn that would have been well known to Will Harvey the Gloucestershire poet. The characters lingering outside the pub have been replaced by motorists seeking a break from the stressful A40. The building has been extended, refurbished and now presents a somewhat nautical appearance. (Photograph by Lockyer).

Out of a former twenty pubs in Newnham only three, including The Ship, are left today. A pub situated on the opposite side of the road named The Rose closed in the eighteenth century, and the landlord moved himself and his business to what is now The Ship Inn. In 1910 the building contained a bar and a billiard room. (Photograph by Lockyer).

Pub Sign. This old pub sign preserved in The Ship shows: Hannah Purnell, Licensed retailer of ale porter and cider. British and Foreign Wines and Spirits etc. Dealer in Tobacco. (Photograph by B. Merrett)

George Inn, Yorkley. The name of the new landlord G. James has been rather crudely painted below the inn sign, and here he stands with his wife and young son outside this very sturdy looking Forest inn. Sadly the site has been redeveloped for housing and the name George Road is the only indication that the pub was ever there. (Photograph by Lockyer).

Queen's Head, Aston Cross. This postcard dated December 1927 was sent by the landlord Thomas Spiers to a Cheltenham wholesaler. A year later the inn was acquired by the Stroud Brewery from Godsells. Situated near Ashchurch the Queens Head has been extended and remains a popular 'port of call'.

Greyhound Inn, Popes Hill. Situated on the fringe of the Forest of Dean this inn presents a relatively modern aspect despite the fact that it was at least a hundred years old when this photograph was taken *c.* 1910. (Photograph by Lockyer)

The same building forty years later shows little change, but since 1950 (the date of the photograph) extensions to the front and rear of the premises have marred its appearance. (Photograph by Adams).

Cross Keys, Marlborough. This old inn became Stroud Brewery property following their take over of W.S. Butler's Marlborough Brewery in 1920. It was demolished and three years later replaced by the impressive building shown below.

The Cross Keys in 1996, closed for many years and now occupied by a firm of stockbrokers. (Photograph by B. Merrett).

The Axe & Cleaver, Much Birch, Hereford. Believed to be of seventeenth century origin, the inn was badly damaged by fire many years ago, and its restoration may account for its somewhat mock Tudor appearance. Nowadays a popular pub restaurant, the building on the left and the orchard behind the car have been cleared away to provide a large parking area. This photograph dates from the early 1950s.

Royal Oak Inn, Wotton Rivers. Situated four miles south of Marlborough this old thatched inn including bakehouse, storehouse and shop was leased in 1937 for twenty-one years by Stroud Brewery Co. from the Master Fellows and Scholars of St John's College, Cambridge at a yearly rental of £50. The premises are basically unaltered but its current popularity has inevitably affected the rustic charm conveyed by this 1950 photograph. (Photograph by Adams)

Horse and Groom, Hereford. In 1927 this inn was acquired by the Stroud Brewery Co. from the Hereford Charity Trustees for £4,433. Now owned by Whitbreads the brickwork has been rendered and the pub sports an attractive pictorial inn sign. The fact that the railings have now disappeared suggests that this is a pre-Second World War photograph.

In Conclusion

I had hoped to find a photograph of one of Stroud Brewery's Welsh pubs such as the Royal Oak at Pencelli, Breconshire to complete this tour, but no luck. Instead I will conclude with a short excerpt from *Wild Wales* by George Borrow whose journeyings made him quite a connoisseur of country inns.

'Being overtaken by another violent shower I thought that we could do no better than shelter ourselves within the public house, and taste the ale. We entered the little hostelry which was one of two or three shabby looking houses standing in contact close by the Ceiriog. In a kind of little back room lighted by a good fire and a window which looked up the valley, we found the landlady, a gentlewoman with a wooden leg who on perceiving me got up from a chair and made me the best curtsey that I ever saw made by a female with such a substitute for a leg of flesh and bone. There were three men seated on a bench by the wall and the other on a settle with a high back which ran from the wall just by the door and shielded those by the fire from the draughts of the doorway'.